THE WAND RING

by Gloria Jean Hughes

Signed Premier Limited Edition
First Printing, November, 1995

Copyright © Country Fair Publishing House 1995

Published by
Country Fair Publishing House
9143 Glover Road, P.O. Box 1167
Fort Langley, B.C. V0J 1J0
Canada 1995
ISBN 0-9699927-0-X

Illustrations by Dan Tolentino

Edited by Jason Hughes

Layout by Impact Printing Services Ltd., Maple Ridge, B.C.

CANADIAN CATALOGUING IN PUBLICATION DATA

Printed in Canada by A.J.A. Printing Ltd., Coquitlam, B.C.

Gloria Jean Hughes

ISBN 0-9699927-0-X

6 1 2 9 5>

9 780969 992707

ACKNOWLEDGEMENTS

Gloria Jean Hughes was born in Vancouver, B.C. Her poetry was exhibited in the Rock Opera "Idealizing Vain Fantasy" published by Country Fair Publishing House. She has written songs which are in the process of being made into a future record album. Over the last two years she has been working on a fiction novel called "Linking Chains", which is based on a true story of three generations of families, who struggle to free themselves and their children from abusive relationships.

The enthusiasm for The Wand Ring came from her son's announcement that he and his wife were expecting their first child. She believes that a birth of a child is a time of renewing the memories of when we were young, of our childhood hopes, dreams and experiences, how we viewed the world. When her children were young, she spent a lot of time reading stories, besides making up her own. Everyone in her family, including friends, encouraged her to put into print the story of "The Wand Ring" for the enjoyment of both children and adults. "Parents pass on their enthusiasm for learning by their example. To experience life through the eyes of a child, is very precious."

Dedicated to our first Grandchild.
Thank you Jason and Lana.

Words and Music written by Charles & Lisa Hughes

CHARACTERS

1. Mother — Middle Aged Woman
2. Daniel — Small Boy
3. Teacher — Story Teller
4. Elven Airies — King of Fairies
5. Centipede — Elven's Secretary
6. Owl — Elven's Wise Advisor
7. Eagle — Head of Castle Guards
8. Mousie — Maid at castle
9. Captain of Cards — Joker Crow
10. Queen Avis — Parrot
11. Blue Fairies — Keystone Police
12. Stone Gaze — Buzzard
13. Toucans — Caribbean Cooks
14. Eerie Cloud — Crystal Ball
15. Daisy Dell — Fairy Princess
16. Lady Twinkle Star — Cleaner
17. Blue Birds — Jazz Singers
18. Canaries — Musicians
19. Hummingbirds — Singers
20. Ace-a-Space — Investigator
21. Jack-of-Parts — Seagull
22. Pink Fairies — Female Police
23. Pumpkins — Telephone Vines
24. Green Frogs — Live in the Well

CONTENTS

CHAPTER ONE — Daniel Meets the Teacher

DANIEL

GYPSY ALLADIN SONG

Once upon a time in a nursery rhyme, there lived a gypsy boy, a young Gypsy Alladin. He played all day, then slept away and he dreamt of many things. Of castles and kings, flying with wings. He dreamt of many things. In his dreams he saw pictures of things, not quite real. He went slipping, sliding, he went tripping, hiding, tripping through his dreams. He went tossing, turning, like a wash machine churning, tripping through his dreams. He dreamt of candy bars and kiddy cars and games of fun and frolic. He dreamt of magic tricks and pick up sticks and play fights with his friends. He dreamt of being a clown, fooling, fooling around and enjoying all the world. But then the sun peeked up, and morning appeared. The dreams they faded away, they soon faded away. Now it's day and he's going to play. Like a merry go round, his dreams, his dreams he found and then they faded away.

This is Daniel's first day of school. His mother is taking one last look at her small son sleeping. Daniel is dreaming of castles and kings in a land of make believe. Stuffed birds and other animal toys lay scattered on his bed. Daniel is awakened by his mother.

Mother: With a smile on her face, mother gently awakens Daniel. *"Daniel! Daniel! Wake Up! This is your first day of school and you mustn't be late. Wake up you sleepy head."*

Daniel: Crawls back under the covers. *"I don't want to go to school I want to stay here, in my bed. Do I have to go?"*

Mother: Mother pulling Daniel out of bed, *"Of course you do! Come on now. You have to get dressed and have your breakfast. I bought you a new outfit and a shiny new lunch kit. There's no time to dilly, dally."* She pulls Daniel out of bed, coaxing him to be happy about the event. She struggles to get his clothes on, with little help from Daniel. *"You'll meet new friends and learn all about the world. You just wait and see, you'll have lots of fun. Now let's get some breakfast into you."*

When they arrive at school, Daniel's mother talks to the teacher, who is wearing a purple dress. The teacher's hair is pulled into a bun, with a pencil protruding from the middle. She wears glasses, and one might say, she's somewhat thin for her height. For a short time, they discuss Daniel's reluctance to come to school. As Daniel's mother begins to leave, Daniel clings to her side, hoping she will take him back home. Reluctantly, and with much reassurance from the teacher, mother leaves.

Daniel is taken to his desk. The teacher returns to the front of the room and begins to give instructions to the class. Daniel puts his head down to rest, while the other children sit at their desks, listening to the teacher. Soon after, the teacher notices that Daniel has fallen asleep at his desk. She walks quietly over to where he is, putting her finger to her mouth to show the children not to make a sound. All the children are giggling and laughing at Daniel. The teacher notices, laying underneath his head, a story book called, "The Wand Ring". She awakens Daniel.

Teacher: Looking sternly, *"Where have you been Daniel?"*

Daniel: Stretching and yawning, suddenly aware of his surroundings, *"I've been to Castle Down County with Ace-a-Space and Stone Gaze, the Wizard."*

Teacher: *"Where is this place? Can we find it on the map? Can I go there? Who are these people? What nonsense!"*

Daniel: *"It's not nonsense, and you're much too tall to go there. Only little folk are allowed to go there."*

Girl: A little girl giggles, *"Can we go there with you?"*

Daniel: *"Yes, we can all go, but we must close our eyes and believe together, so we don't get lost."*

Boy: *"Sure we can. How do we get there then? Fly?"* laughs holding his belly.

Daniel: Looking upset, *"Only if you believe you can! We could go there today, if you want!"* Turning to the teacher he asks, *"Would it be okay with you if we all go to Castle Down today?"*

Teacher: Raising an eyebrow, *"How do we get there? We have no transportation, silly boy."*

Daniel: Excited at the prospect, all the children gather around his desk. Daniel answers excitedly, *"All we have to do is sit in a circle and hold hands. Then we must close our eyes and wish while you read The Wand Ring to us."*

The teacher, seeing how excited the class was about this opportunity to travel, reads the story.

Teacher: *"Oh, all right then, if I must."* She takes the story book from Daniel and proceeds to the front of the class. She tells the class to come to the front and make a circle on the floor. *"Hurry! Hurry! Before we run out of time."* After they were all settled down she asks everyone to hold hands and close their eyes. She begins to read .... Slowly.

CHAPTER TWO — Visit to County Down Kingdom

"Once upon a time, in a fantasy rhyme, there lived a castle kingdom, rich in elven lore. Somewhere outside reality, in an animated galaxy where elated little folk dwell, and they lived very happily."

The children's imaginations begin to envision the story as if they were actually there. A vision appears, right in the middle of the circle. Even though the children have their eyes closed, inside their minds, each one was seeing the same thing.

All the children could see a pumpkin patch, with a large tree that held many different shaped bird houses. Right in the middle of the tree was a large bird house that resembled a castle. There were pumpkin vines running all over the ground and a small wishing well. On the ground and in the air, one could see all kinds of little folk going about their business.

The teacher continues, unaware of what was happening in the circle.

ELVEN KING OF THE FAIRIES

"And it came to pass that Elven Airies was King of the Fairies, King of Castle Down County. Keeper of the Cable-carts, Reeper of the Rabble-rorts, but apparently, Elf was in a quandary, for it seems Elf lost his wand-ring"

The vision changes to the inside of the Bird Castle. In the office of the castle is a large elderly Golden winged fairy. He has a crown on his head, and is walking around rubbing his chin, looking very nervous and concerned. Little moonbeam lamp shades follow him around as he paces back and forth.

Elven Airies: Yelling to his secretary through a pumpkin intercom. *"Send for Big Cheese Checker Charts, and Captain of the cards! Send for the head of hearts, and all the other Rabble-rorts, to help find the Ring-of-Rorts!"*

Centipede: Sitting at a lady bug desk, in the outer hallway, filing her many nails answers, *"Yes your Royal Highness. Right away!"* She calls through a pumpkin loudspeaker, *"Will Big Cheese Checker Charts and Captain of the Cards and all the other head Rabble-rorts report to the King's office, immediately!"*

the CROW   the EAGLE

A white bearded Eagle known as Checker Charts, flies into the room and stands by the desk in the office. He is the head of the guards at the castle and keeps watch over the inhabitants of County Down.

The Joker Crow, who is in charge of the Comedy Club, and Ace of Hearts, a Turtle Dove, who is the local Relationship Therapist, come strolling into the office.

The Joker is laughing and telling jokes to Turtle Dove. The Owl, who is advisor to the King, comes into the room where everyone is waiting. He is holding a list of things to do, looking over his glasses at King Elven. The moonbeams follow whoever is moving in the room.

Owl: *"I just don't know where we can look. I've searched the whole castle through and there just is no sign of your ring. Who? Who could have seen where you lost it? Who? Who?"*

Elven: *"It must be here somewhere. I remember leaving it right here, on my desk. It can't have gone far. Checker Charts have you come up with any ideas?"*

Checker Charts: *"Sorry your*

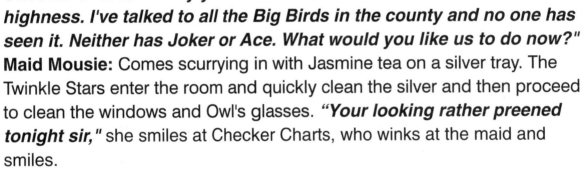

THE OWL

highness. I've talked to all the Big Birds in the county and no one has seen it. Neither has Joker or Ace. What would you like us to do now?"

Maid Mousie: Comes scurrying in with Jasmine tea on a silver tray. The Twinkle Stars enter the room and quickly clean the silver and then proceed to clean the windows and Owl's glasses. *"Your looking rather preened tonight sir,"* she smiles at Checker Charts, who winks at the maid and smiles.

Joker Crow: Laughing at Checker Charts behaviour, *"Now don 't go getting soft on little Miss Mousie. She's just trying to trap you into getting your feathers in a flutter. She always flatters the Big Cheese's."*

Elven: *"We have to do something. Gather all the Rabble-rorts together, maybe they can help with the search. Just can't bare to have to tell the Queen of Rorts. This is a very special Wish ring she had made for the princess. She wants to give it to her at her Birthday Party. What will I do? What will I do?"* The Owl flies over to the Joker and Ace of Hearts and discuss the situation with them.

Owl: *"Who? Who can we get to help with this search? Who? Who? We must keep this a secret. This was a special gift to be given to the Princess for her birthday. No one must know. No one! Especially Queen Avis!"*

QUEEN OF RORTS

Checker Charts and Joker, both shake their heads and put their hands over their mouth. They walk off down the hall, checking corners, under rugs, inside musical instruments, whispering, ***"Sh, Sh, Sh, we mustn't tell the Queen, Sh, Sh, Sh, we mustn't tell the....."*** Suddenly, they look up and there she comes all dressed regal like. She's in a hurry, heading for the King's office. They try to get out of her way, by hiding in the corners.

CHAPTER THREE — The Queen Appears

"The Queen of Rorts appeared, really regal rebel roused, because the king's daughter, Daisy Dell, was crying by the wishing well."

Queen: Walking in a hurry down the castle hallway, complaining. *"I just don't know what has gotten into that girl She sits there crying, crying, crying."* She looks out the window of the castle, down at Daisy Dell. *"Her colours have changed from bright to blue. These should be the happiest days of her life. Haven't I been a concerned fairy God-mother? Hasn't she had the best of things. She even has her own vine to talk to her friends. Her generation never seems satis*fied." Shaking her head. Looking out the corner of her eyes, raising one eyebrow she notices Joker and Ace, hiding in the corners. *"What are you two hiding for? What are you up to? You look awfully suspicious. Well goodbye Joker! How are you Ace?"* She continues walking by them unconcerned as to why they are hiding, having no time to listen to their answers. She walks by the centipede and bursts into Elven's office, unannounced.

Elven: Looking under his desk, under his chair. Suddenly, he is aware of the Queen's presence. Acting very nervous, he turns to face her. *"Your Majesty, what a pleasure! Can I get you a ring, I mean a chair? Why are you here? What have you heard? It's not true!"*

Queen: *"I'm here to pick up Daisy Dell's wand ring. I want everything to be ready for her birthday party. I've arranged for all the Birds to come and entertain us on that night. She loves the Blue's Birds. I've asked them to sing some of her favourite songs. Maybe listening to them will make her feel good enough to sing. I don't really approve of their singing, too noisy for me. The Buzzard has agreed to do all of the catering, he's such a whiz at cooking. Now where is that ring?"* Trying to look around Elven, who is backed up against his lady bug desk.

Elven: *"I sent it out to the Twinkle Stars for cleaning. That's right! I sent it out for cleaning. Don't you worry, it will be back in time for the party."*

Queen: *"It better be! I don't want anything to go wrong. I have no time to waste. There is so much to do. Wasting time, got to go. People to meet, things to do. No time for silly things."* She turns and quickly walks out, acting irritated. As she rushes down the hallway, she kicks at the small creatures that get in her way. She has no patience for wasting time.

TIME THIEVES SONG

Time thieves are crime thieves, snatching away the best of the day. Yes, wasting away is an untimely prey for reepers and weepers and untimely keepers. Knocking you out, you try to outshout. You give with a right in an untimely fight. Gremlins and Monsters, uncomely creatures, pulling you apart, you can't make a start. You kick with a shoe, to try and undo. What's taken away is the best of the day. Time thieves are crime thieves and like a blight they steal the whole night. If you know what I'm talking about, "Shout Get Out! Get out of bed hey sleepy head!" Time thieves are crime thieves, snatching away the best of the day.

Elven: Calls Joker and Checker Charts who rush back into his office, *"Summon all of Castle Down! We've got to find the ring. Got to help your King! Get Daisy Dell to sing, and appease the Queen."* Elven picks up his pumpkin telephone and calls the Blue Fairy headquarters.
Blue Fairy: Sitting in the Bird Station, wearing a police hat, answers the pumpkin vine, *"Hello! Fairy Investigations! How can I help you?"*
Elven: *"This is Elven, King of the Fairies. I'm in a lot of trouble and need all the help I can get. I've lost the wand ring that Queen Avis was going to give to Princess Daisy Dell I need to find it before the birthday party next month. You've got to send out a search party."*
Blue Fairy: *"Right-a-way your highness! "* He calls over to the Queen Bee and informs her of the problem. The Queen Bee flies off to her hive, the florist shop. The honeybees are buzzing, arranging flowers for deliveries. She informs the honeybees of what has happened, and all the bees start buzzing around looking for the ring in all the blossoms.

CHAPTER FOUR — Hunting for the Wand Ring

"There were Blue Fairies, Pink Fairies, Snow Fairies, Twinkle Stars, searching for the ring. Got to help the King! There were Moon Beams, Lady Bugs, Hummingbirds, Honeybees searching for the ring. Got to help the King! There were Pink Bunnies, White Mice, Canaries and Bluebirds searching for the ring. Got to help the King! There were Pumpkins, Butterflies, Ponies and a wise Old Owl, searching for the ring. Got to help the King."

All of the inhabitants begin to look for the wand ring. They sing while they walk along, peeking under flowers, looking in the grass and under bushes.

the PINK FAIRIES

DING-A-LING SONG

I love bells, ding-a-ling bells. Ding, Ding, Ring, Ring, ding-a-ling bells. I love chimes, churchy chimes. Ding, Ding, Ring, Ring, ding-a-ling chimes. Door bells swing, ding-a-long dong. Ding, Ding, Ring, Ring, ding-a-long gong. Ding-a-long ring, ding-a-long dong. You can hear my ding-a-long song. Ring, Ring, Ding, Ding, ding-a-long song. You can hear my sing-a-long song. Dogs that bark, the sound of a lark, a mouse in the attic, the sound of static. The honk of a horn, popping of corn. The train goes toot, who gives a hoot! Westminster chimes, silly rhymes. Piccolo, or flute, who gives a hoot! I love bells, ding-a-long bells. I loves chimes, churchy chimes. Ding, Ding, Ring, Ring, ding-a-long bells.

Owl: Three weeks later Owl flies into Elven's office. *"Who? Who have you got looking for that darn ring?"*

Elven: *"Everyone in the County. Nothing has been found, there is only a week before the party. I know I'm going to be de-winged. The Queen called and is very concerned about my daughter Daisy Dell. Every day she sits by the well and cries. I just don't understand girls. Why does she have to get so emotional all the time? The Queen believes the Wand Ring is the only thing that will make her happy. It's suppose to be a special Wishing Ring. What will I do? What will I do?"* Elven paces back and forth.

Owl: *"Maybe the Wizard could see! Stone Gaze has a magic mirror ball, for the future it could tell. Who? Who?"*

Elven: *"Now, maybe he could piece it all. I'll give him a call!"* Elven picks up his pumpkin and calls Stone Gaze. The pumpkin rings in the Buzzard's laboratory.

The vision changes to a laboratory full of dark things. A zodiac and astro charts hang on the wall, old trunks, clocks, wizards hats, glass mirror balls, spiders and webs. Daniel is gazing into the magic mirror ball, not paying any attention to the ringing phone. The Buzzard, in a chef's uniform, with flour all over him, yells at the boy.

Stone Gaze: *"Daniel! Wake up! Wake up! You can't just sit there and dream. There is more to be done. Now, wake up and pay attention! I've food to make for the party and there isn't time to gaze. There will be times to dream of castles and kings and far away places later. Answer the phone!"*

Daniel: *"Sorry! Sorry! I guess I just got lost in my dreams. It feels like I'm travelling to new countries far away. I just close my eyes and I can see anything I want, I can be anywhere, anyone."*

Stone Gaze: *"Stop your mind from dreaming boy. Answer the phone!"* To himself, *"Such a lazy boy. He'll never learn anything if he doesn't pay attention. I don't know what I can do with him. He just doesn't seem to fit around here."* Mumbling he picks up some more baking goods and goes back to the kitchen. *"Dreams, humbug! You are what you are, only potions can change that. Dreams, such nonsense."*

Daniel: Answering the phone, *"Hello! Is anybody still there? Hello!"*

Elven: *"This is the King of the Fairies calling. I need to speak to the Wizard. Hurry! Hurry!"*

Daniel: Calls to Stone Gaze, who is preparing food, *"The pumpkin's for you Wizard. Hurry! Hurry! It's the King of the Fairies."*

Stone Gaze is in the kitchen, preparing all kinds of food for the party. Mice are scurrying around helping him. The Caribbean Toucans are cooking, singing, dancing and bumping each other. All the cauldrons are boiling and bubbling while they dance around stirring the pots and rattling the pans. All sorts of bird seed, vegetables and fruits are waiting to be made into some delicious party foods, for the anticipated guests.

Stone Gaze: *Picks up the pumpkin, "Wizard here. What's the hurry?"*
Elven: *"You must help me find the Ring-a-rort. The Queen is expecting me to bring it to the party and I've searched everywhere and it's nowhere to be found. You're my last hope. Look in your magic mirror ball and tell me what you see."*
The Toucans begin singing:

TOPSY TURVEY WORLD SONG

It's a topsy turvey world, it's a topsy turvey world. Tossing and turning, churning and burning, topsy turvey world. Where's your place in this human race and is there peace, is there compassion? Is there life everlasting? It's a topsy turvey world. Swirling, twirling, unfurling elements. Life's a spooked herd of elephants. It's a topsy turvey world, it's a topsy turvey world. A mad cap comedy of keystone cops. A topsy turvey world. What goes up, must come down and life it's a turn-a-round. Turn, turn, turn-around. Inner earth, outer feelings, inner peace, outer passion. Out of place, out of fashion. Around and around and around we go. Up and down like a circus clown. It's a topsy turvey world, it's a topsy turvey world. Frothing, flowing, bubbling, boiling. Life's a hassle a rat race wrestle. Outer space, inner dealings. It's a topsy turvey world.

Stone Gaze: Mumbles to himself about how people expect too much of wizards, *"One moment please."* He pushes Daniel away from the ball. All the mice, and the three Toucans stop what they are doing to watch the wizard at work. He takes off his chef hat and puts on his magic hat and begins. He stares into the magic ball and recites:

        "With a slip and a slap and a rap-a-tap-tap, a skippy-dippity-dippity-do, magic ball do your thing, show me where to find the ring."

A grey eerie vision appears in the ball singing back to Stone Gaze for direction:

WHICH A WAY SONG

Stone Gaze: *"Hey, hey which a way, got to find the light of day. Hey, hey which away, got to find a place to stay."
Eerie Cloud: "Soul seer, mind freer, tell me no line, show me a sign."
Stone Gaze: "I'll show you a sign, I'll tell you no line."
Eerie Cloud: "Fortune teller, time zone dweller, prophesize and tell no lies."
Stone Gaze: "I'll prophesize and tell you no lies."
Eerie Cloud: "Sorcerer, magic man, give me a hand, map out a plan."
Stone Gaze: "I'll map out a plan, I'll give you a hand."
Eerie Cloud: "Wise as a wizard, rich in the mind, my astro chart you soon can find. To forecast the future, predict the time, in your crystal ball these things you will find. Reflect on my life, my conscience and strife, I want you to know which way to go."*

Stone Gaze: After enquiring of the Eerie Cloud the whereabouts of the Wand Ring, Stone Gaze comes back to the pumpkin phone and tells Elven what was shown to him in the crystal ball. *"All I see is Daisy Dell, crying by the wishing well. There's a small jar with a twinkle star and a frog sitting beside her. They seem to be singing. No Wand Ring is to be seen."*

Daisy Dell and Lady Twinkle Star sing to each other of their loneliness:

LIKE A LONELY STAR SONG

Daisy Dell: *"I can hear you coming, but someone has closed the door. I know your out there, somewhere, this isn't really fair."

Twinkle Star: "I can hear you coming, but I'm in a dark place where there is no trace. I'm like a stone, I'm all alone."

Daisy Dell: "Long days and many years. All grey with many tears. I'm like a lonely star trapped in a jar. Locked up tight with no light."

Twinkle Star: "I might as well dig a grave, in a deep dark cave. For I can't see the grace of your lovely face."

Daisy Dell: "Please free me from these dreams, these shackles that I feel. Let me see that you are real, really real."

Twinkle Star: "I can't twinkle, I can't shine. I have no one to call mine."

Daisy Dell: "I'm like a lonely star, searching for where you are. I can feel you near but I know you're far."*

CHAPTER FIVE — Ace-of-Space Arrives

"Now 30 odd days have past, from the first day to last. Since the King lost his wand-ring. Where could it be? Maybe, the Wizard could see! Stone Gaze had a magic mirror ball for the future he could tell. Now, maybe he could piece it all, but all he saw was Daisy Dell, crying by the wishing well............. In the meantime, to carry on our fantasy rhyme, there was a princely keeper, from another County Down. His name was Ace-a-Space with his trusty friend Jack-of-Parts. They came to help the Rabble-rorts."

Ace-a-Space arrives in town wearing air goggles and a silver uniform with planets and stars. His friend, Jack-of-Parts, who likes to repair everything, has nuts, bolts and tools projecting from his carpenter coveralls. They are Special Investigators, sent for by the Blue Fairies. They arrive during the parade, in the Hop-a-Long Taxi service. The Blue Snail is pulling a cart with the Blue Birds who are singing one of their favourite jazz tunes, "Can You Rhyme.'" A Green Snail pulls the Green Canaries who play guitar, clarinet and saxophone. The Red Snail is pulling the female singers, the Hummingbirds. There are Centipede clowns dressed as cowboys. The onlookers are various County Down inhabitants including white mice, snow fairies, twinkle stars, blue and pink fairies. The Hummingbirds are humming:

CAN YOU RHYME SONG

*It's not a crime, if you can't rhyme. I got a rhythm and a rhyme. A dollar and a dime. Got the time and I can't climb. I got a tingling spine. Can you mime? Can you rhyme? Well skip along and join my song. With a slip and a slap and a rap, tap, tap. Can you clap? Can you rhyme. What's your sign? What's yours is mine. A string in time saves nine. I am caught in a bind, your very kind. Your very, very kind. I've got a bottle of thyme, I crossed the line. Left behind. Life is fine, life is fine. Skippity, dippity, dippity do. I'll do the soft shoe with you. It's not a crime if you can't rhyme. I got a rhythm and a rhyme. A dollar and a dime. *

ACE-A-SPACE and JACK OF PARTS

Ace-a-Space: Talking to Jack-of-Parts, "*We must report to the Blue Fairies Police Station as soon as the parade is over. We have only a couple of days to find this Wand Ring.*"

Jack-of-Parts: *"Right you are captain! I've brought all the investigative equipment with me, so we can get started right away. We'll have this case solved in no time. You can count on me!"*

After the parade they both fly up to the Bird Station to talk to the Blue and Pink Fairies, to see how the investigation is going.

"The deck was dealt, the cards up faced. Who could answer where the ring was placed? But it came to be, no ring was there to see."

Pink Fairy: "*You're our last hope! We've looked everywhere, but not a trace of the Wand Ring. Not even the Wizard could tell. The Birthday party is in two days. What are we going to tell Elven, King of the Fairies?*"

Ace-a-Space: "*Give me all the facts. Where was everyone at the time the ring went missing? There must be a clue.*" They discuss the situation among themselves.

Jack-of-Parts: "*Let me use some of my equipment to help Elven remember.*" He pulls out a magnifying glass, "*I know I have something here that will bring back the time.*" Searching, clumsily dropping tools, finally finding a clock.

Ace-a-Space: "*Who is this Daisy Dell? Why is she always crying? She must know something of this. We will have to go speak to her.*"

Blue Fairy: "*Right away, sir! I'll arrange for the Butterflies to escort you over to the castle tomorrow morning. Tonight you are to be our guest at the Crow's Comedy Club. You'll enjoy the show he puts on. He's a real card.*"

After the show, Ace-a-Space returns to his room, alone. He looks out his port hole at the moon and stars and dreams of one day meeting his dream girl. Wondering when. He envisions what she will look like, floating in the sky.

Ace begins to sing a song about his illusionary love:

I AM A DREAMER SONG

I sit here looking at the stars, wondering where you are. Wishing you were thinking of me. Hoping you will be my only true love. But you are still but a dream. You will never know how far our love will go. How much I love you so, I am a dreamer, you are my dream. Reality is so far between. I am a dreamer you are my dream. What I've seen and where I've been. It's all an illusionary scene. Just an illusionary dream. Like the bird up in the tree, you must be free to fly in the sky. If you return, I'll know it's forever. Have you ever dreamt a dream. To try and make it real. This is exactly how I feel, how I feel. I am a dreamer, you are my dream. Reality is so far between, you're just an illusionary dream, just an illusionary scheme.

In the morning, the Butterflies arrive to take Ace, Jack and the Blue Fairy over to the Castle. Elven meets them at the castle's main port hole and after discussing the importance of finding the wand ring with Ace, he takes them down to the garden where Ace-a-Space sees beautiful Daisy Dell sitting, crying by the wishing well. He immediately becomes smitten by her beauty. This is the girl he has dreamt of all his life. His heart begins to beat, loudly. He walks over to her and kneels down and kisses her hand.

Ace-a-Space: *"I'm honoured to meet you princess. May I ask you why such a pretty lady like yourself sits here all day crying?"*
Daisy Dell: Stops crying and looks at the prince. Remembering her wish, she smiles, *"I'm so blue. I took my father's Wand Ring and don't know what to do. I accidently dropped it down the wishing well and the Frog refuses to give it back."* Looking down the well at the Frog she tells him the story, *"At one time he was a Twinkle Star, but he wasn't happy being small. He stole some potion from the Wizard and it turned him into a green Frog. Until the Wizard sets him free, my father's wand-ring I'll never see."* She begins to weep again and runs off.

Ace-a-Space: Turns and talks to Jack-of-Parts, *"I will go and talk to the Wizard and explain everything. I'm sure there is some way to undo this spell You stay here and try to coax the Frog into giving back the ring. I'll go over and talk to the King, to hear what he has to say about this matter."*
Jack-of-Parts: Discusses the matter with the Frog, *"I'm sure we can find some compromise to this mess."* After pulling out a puzzle board, with one piece missing, he asks the Frog, *"Give me all the facts."*

CHAPTER SIX — The Wand Ring is Found

The Frog tells Jack-of-Parts that he was holding the Wand Ring until Daisy Dell could get the Wizard to change him back into a Twinkle Star. Apparently, Daisy Dell had taken the Wand Ring from her father's office, without asking. She knew it had some special power to make wishes come true. Daisy Dell had wished for a Prince to call and then accidently dropped the wand ring down into the wishing well. Frog thought he could use the powers for himself but it would only work for the one who owns it. Jack and Ace discuss what the Frog has said.

"Now the princely Ace-a-Space had a fancy for sweet Daisy Dell He found her at the wishing well. It seems, she had lost the Wand Ring, when wishing for a prince to call. She dropped it in the wishing well and she was too afraid to tell."

Ace-a-Space: Goes over and talks to Elven, *"We must get the Wizard to change Frog back into a Twinkle Star and release his girlfriend from the jar."*

Elven calls the Buzzard over to the pumpkin patch. He explains to the Buzzard what has happened. The Buzzard informs Elven and Ace of what the Frog has done.

Stone Gaze: *"The male Twinkle Star had stolen some of my potions. He had thought he could change himself into a Big Star. Instead, he used the wrong formula. Now he's a Frog, and rightly so! Unless he is willing to accept responsibility for his actions, he will remain a Frog. That is how the spell works. And until he tells me where the potion is, his little girl friend will remain in the jar. It's all up to the Frog. But he chooses to remain stubborn. He wants it all or nothing at all. Even if it means the female Twinkle Star must remain in the jar. I will agree to return the Frog back, under conditions .....that he returns the potions he stole from me and accepts who he is and promises to never again steal from others to try and change himself."*

Ace-a-Space: *"I will go and talk to the Frog. I'm sure we can work things out."*

Ace-a-Space returns to the well and informs Frog of what the Wizard has told him. Frog accepts his responsibility for his actions, but he doesn't trust the Wizard. Frog informs Ace-a-Space that he will return the potions to him for safe keeping. The Wizard may have the potion back, only after he is returned to a Twinkle Star and his girlfriend is released from the jar. Ace-a-Space returns to the pumpkin patch and confirms this arrangement with the Wizard. The Wizard flies to the wishing well and is greeted by Jack-of-Parts, Ace-a-Space and all the other Rabble-rorts who are handling the case, stand by, waiting for King Elven to join them.

Elven: Talks to the Buzzard, *"I'm really sorry to take you away from all your preparations, but everything hinges on you. The Queen of Rorts is waiting up in my office for the Wand Ring and the celebrations can't begin, as long as Daisy Dell is crying in her room."*

Stone Gaze: *"I'll do what I can, your Highness. Hopefully, this medicine will work."*

The Buzzard gives just the right amount of medicine to the Frog, then stares down into the well and recites:

> *"With a slip and a slap, and a rap-a-tap-tap,*
> *Drink this medicine and it will change you back!*
> *Be proud of who and what you are,*
> *That's the only magic, in being a Big Star."*

The Frog drinks the Wizards potion and is changed back into a Twinkle Star. Then the Wizard releases Lady Twinkle Star from the jar. They both fly up into the air, twinkling. Happy to be set free. Ace-a-Space returns the missing potions to the Wizard. After a moment, the male Twinkle Star remembers his promise and returns the wand-ring to the King.

> *"Summon all of castle down. The Prince found the wand-ring. He went to tell the King. He got Daisy Dell to sing, and helped appease the Queen."*

Everyone begins arriving for the Birthday party, held down by the wishing well. Ace-a-Space arrives and escorts the Princess to the celebration. The Queen sits on her lady bug throne while the King of the Fairies stands at her side. Ace-a-Space presents Daisy Dell with her royal wand ring, a special gift from the Queen. The Blue Birds are singing with the Hummingbirds, while the Canaries play their instruments. Stone Gaze and the white mice are busy serving everyone. The Bees are buzzing around, arranging the flowers.

the BUZZARD

During the celebrations Daniel decides that he wants to return to school. He goes over to Stone Gaze and asks him for help in returning. Stone Gaze is pleased to hear of Daniel's decision. He tells Daniel that when he learns to read, he can come back to County Down anytime, if only in his mind. Stone Gaze hands the Wand Ring book back to Daniel who begins to slowly fade away from the Birthday party. His dream fades back to the classroom while the Blue Birds sing:

ODDESSY BAND SONG

We're the Oddessy band. We're from the twelfth of never land. We're a hard driving, hip jiving, Rock and Roll machine. We know where we're coming from and where we've been. We're gonna make the scene or somewhere in between. We've descended from a cloud. You think we are loud! You ought to hear our other ship. Ohh.. what a trip. Bet you'd flip, I'm hip. We are the Oddessy band from the twelfth of never land. We're the music masters, forecasters, rock and roll machine. We're the Oddessy band from the twelfth of never land.

In the classroom the teacher sits with a raised eyebrow, a closed book on her lap. She looks around at all of the children who have fallen asleep. In the middle of the circle sits a small round pumpkin.

Teacher: She smiles and recites in a soft voice.....

> *"With a slip and a slap,*
> *And a rap-a-tap-tap,*
> *Send that little pumpkin back!"*

Suddenly, the pumpkin disappears.....all that is left is a puff of smoke.